TV Remotes

Robin Koontz

rourkeeducationalmedia.com

Scan for Related Titles
and Teacher Resources

Teaching Focus:
Fluency: Using Expression- Have students read aloud to practice reading with expression and with appropriate pacing.

Before Reading:

Building Academic Vocabulary and Background Knowledge
Before reading a book, it is important to set the stage for your child or student by using pre-reading strategies. This will help them develop their vocabulary, increase their reading comprehension, and make connections across the curriculum.

1. *Read the title and look at the cover. Let's make predictions about what this book will be about.*
2. *Take a picture walk by talking about the pictures/photographs in the book. Implant the vocabulary as you take the picture walk. Be sure to talk about the text features such as headings, the Table of Contents, glossary, bolded words, captions, charts/diagrams, or index.*
3. *Have students read the first page of text with you then have students read the remaining text.*
4. *Strategy Talk – use to assist students while reading.*
   - *Get your mouth ready*
   - *Look at the picture*
   - *Think…does it make sense*
   - *Think…does it look right*
   - *Think…does it sound right*
   - *Chunk it – by looking for a part you know*
5. *Read it again.*
6. *After reading the book complete the activities below.*

Content Area Vocabulary
Use glossary words in a sentence.

channel
infrared
radio waves
receiver
remote
signal

After Reading:

Comprehension and Extension Activity
After reading the book, work on the following questions with your child or students in order to check their level of reading comprehension and content mastery.

1. *Explain the purpose of a receiver. (Summarize)*
2. *What was the first remote called? (Summarize)*
3. *What functions does your TV remote have? (Text to self connection)*
4. *What is the difference between infrared remotes and non-infrared remotes? (Asking questions)*

Extension Activity
Look around your home. How many different remotes can you find? Do you have one for the TV, DVD player, CD player, ceiling fan, or toy truck? Now compare and contrast the remotes. How are they alike and how are they different? Can some be used through walls while others can't? How do these remotes make your life easier?

Table of Contents

What Is a TV Remote?

The first TV **remote** was called Lazy Bones. People could control the TV without getting out of the chair!

Lazy Bones had a wire that led to the TV.

It controlled the TV through the wire.

Today, TV remotes do not have a wire.

Some TVs don't even work without a remote. So be sure you don't lose it!

The first wireless TV remote was called the Flash-Matic.

Button Action

A remote control has buttons.

Lots of things have a remote control to make them work.

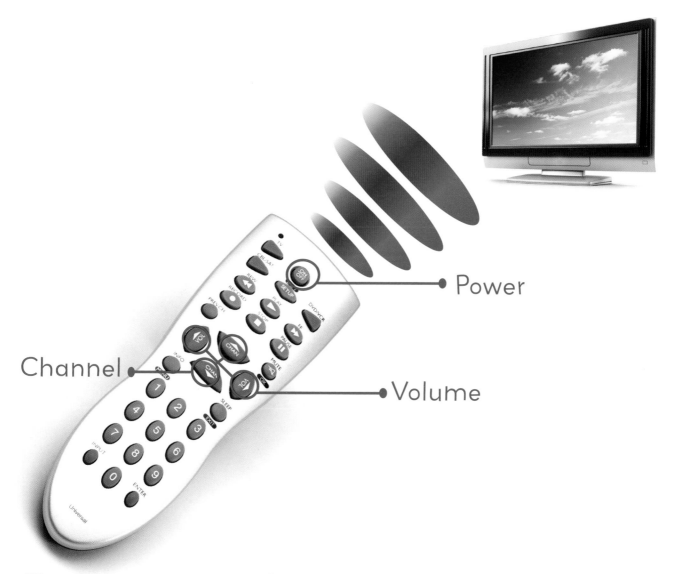

Power

Channel

Volume

Each button sends a different message to the TV. The buttons are marked to tell what they do.

A button's job may be to change the **channel.** It may control the sound. It may turn the TV on or off.

Point and Push!

When a button is pushed, it touches a part inside the remote control.

Power Button

Pushing a button tells the remote control to send a **signal** to the TV.

An **infrared** light on the remote carries the signal.

The TV has a **receiver.**

Some remote controls can control many devices, such as a TV, sound system, or DVD player.

The receiver understands the remote's message. It tells the TV what to do.

The TV remote must be pointed at the TV receiver.

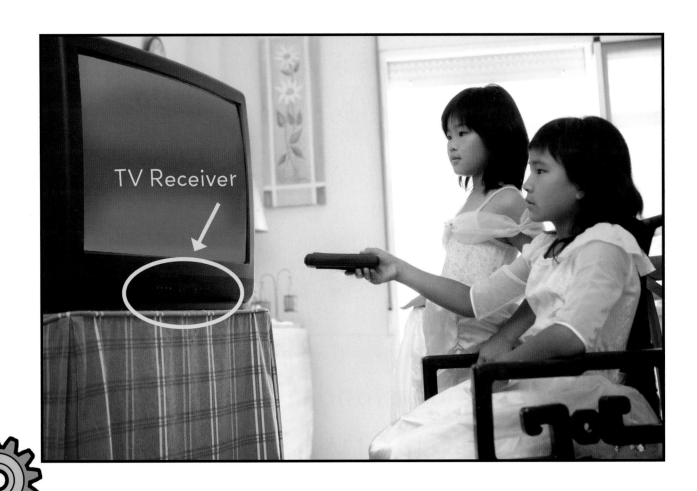

TV Receiver

An infrared remote can't see through walls or other objects.

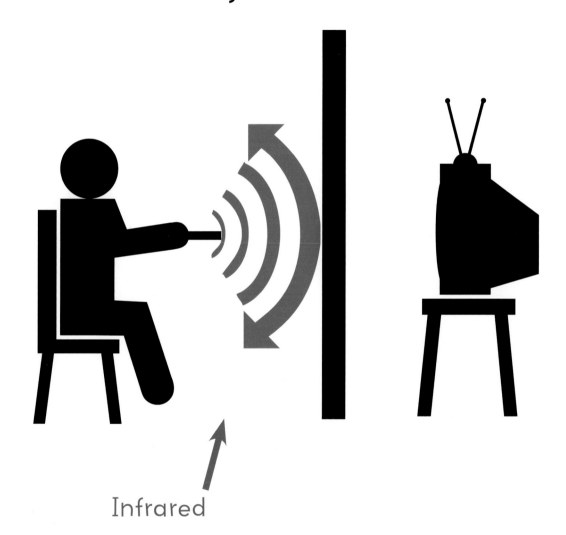

Infrared

See-Through Remote

Another kind of TV remote does not use infrared light.

It sends its message using **radio waves.**

This kind of TV remote can see through walls!

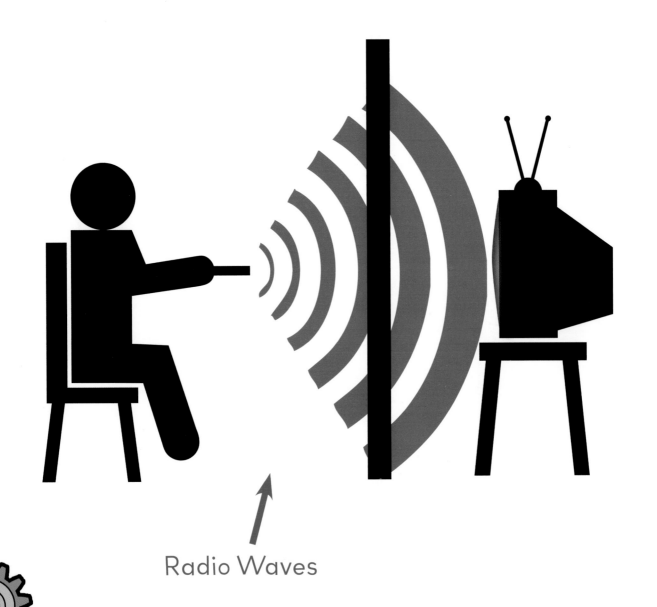

Radio Waves

From Lazy Bones to smartphones,
TV remotes make life easier!

Smartphones and tablets have apps that work like TV remote controls.

Photo Glossary

channel (CHAN-uhl): A TV or radio station.

infrared (in-fruh-RED): Rays of light that cannot be seen and are longer than rays that produce red light.

radio waves (RAY-dee-oh WAYVZ): Waves that can send signals through the air.

 **receiver** (ri-SEE-vur): The part of a device, such as a TV, that collects a signal.

 **remote** (ri-MOHT): A device that controls a machine, especially a television or VCR, from a distance.

 **signal** (SIG-nuhl): Something that is sent out for radio, TV, or telephone communication.

Index

Websites to Visit

www.whyzz.com/how-do-remote-controls-work

scienceofthecity.net/2011/?p=485

electronics.howstuffworks.com/inside-rc.htm

About the Author

Robin Koontz is an author and illustrator of a wide variety of books and articles for children and young adults. After writing this book, she has a new appreciation for her TV remote control. She lives with her husband in the Coast Range of western Oregon.

Meet The Author!
www.meetREMauthors.com

© 2015 Rourke Educational Media

www.rourkeeducationalmedia.com

PHOTO CREDITS: Cover © nexus7 ; title page, 10, 15 © monkeybusinessimages; page 5, 7 © Zenith Electronics LLC; page 6, 23 © mattbaker; page 8 © goh siok hian; page 9 © koele; page 1 © Craig Lopetz; page 12 © Andrew Howe; page 14, 22 © Andrey Popov; page 16, 23 © Luanamarina; page 17, 20 © Miguel Angel Salines Salinas; page 18, 22 © Sanjay Deva; page 19 © grekoff; page 21, 23 © skynesher; page 22 © Jen Thomas

Edited by: Jill Sherman

Cover design by: Nicola Stratford, nicolastratford.com

Interior design by: Jen Thomas

Library of Congress PCN Data

TV Remotes/ Robin Koontz
(How It Works)
ISBN (hard cover)(alk. paper) 978-1-62717-642-2
ISBN (soft cover) 978-1-62717-764-1
ISBN (e-Book) 978-1-62717-884-6
Library of Congress Control Number: 2014934209
Printed in the United States of America, North Mankato, Minnesota

Also Available as:

ROURKE'S
e-Books